YOU AND THE LAW
OVERSEAS

AMERICAN FORCES INFORMATION SERVICE • DEPARTMENT OF DEFENSE
1989

Contents

3   Introduction

7   NATO Status of Forces Agreement

10   Criminal Jurisdiction

14   Custody of the Accused

16   Rights of the Accused

18   Other Safeguards

21   Confinement in Foreign Prisons

23   Status of U.S. Forces in Other Countries

28   Legal Status of Offices of Defense
      Cooperation and Military Missions

30   Status of Civilian Employees and
      Dependents

32   Status of Forces Agreements and
      Foreign Claims

INTRODUCTION

Overseas duty can be one of the most challenging and rewarding aspects of military service. Both the service member and, in the case of accompanied tours, the military family are provided with opportunities to travel, to learn new languages, to experience new sights and sounds and to meet people of other countries and cultures. At the same time, U.S. forces personnel and their families get a firsthand opportunity to see how people of other lands perceive and react to the United States and its citizens.

There are also hardships and some inconveniences associated with a tour of duty in a foreign country. In the case of unaccompanied tours, the hardships of separation hit both those who remain at home and those who leave. When a family goes overseas, there are the problems of becoming familiar with the new surroundings, perhaps a different language and learning how "things are done" in a different country.

In most cases, the "plusses" outweigh the "minuses," and a tour of duty in a foreign country turns out to be an enjoyable, broadening experience.

As you plan and look forward to your overseas tour, there is one thing you should give particular attention to in advance, aside from all the hassle of moving your belongings and completing the travel. This special area of consideration is the new relationship you will experience with the law and law enforcement officials of foreign countries, both in the country to which you will be assigned and in those you may visit on duty or leave.

Most Americans in uniform and their dependents have had few encounters with "the law" except through television and the movies, news accounts and other indirect sources. At home, we are in one sense surrounded by laws and regulations that govern our conduct, both civilian and military. The difference between "right" and "wrong," between conforming to the law and breaking it, is usually quite clear.

Although some people would say we have too many laws, the fact is that most of our laws are based on our own customs, traditions, history and current viewpoints on how people should conduct themselves. Thus, in our day-to-day lives, "the law" is nothing unusual because it is built on practices and rules we are familiar with and respect.

When we do need legal guidance or if we should break the law, there are familiar mechanisms (which are themselves part of the law of the land) through which we may seek assistance or under which we are guaranteed certain rights, protections and considerations. Perhaps nowhere else in the world is the individual as thoroughly protected by constitutional and other legal guarantees as when he or she crosses paths with "the law" in the United States.

On your overseas tour of duty, the relationships between you and "the law" will undergo a significant change. While military personnel remain subject to the Uniform Code of Military Justice and to all U.S. laws that apply outside the country, there is a new, very important element for you to understand. In a foreign country, depending upon the type of agreement that exists between the host government and the United States government, you may be subject to the laws of that country.

The laws in your host country more than likely developed in the same way as laws in the United States— that is, based on custom, tradition, practice, necessity and experience. However, in many cases the customs and history are far different from those to which you are accustomed, and so are the laws.

If this is your first overseas duty and the first time your family has traveled or lived outside the United

States, it will also mark the first time you and they have come under the jurisdiction of a foreign legal system.

This booklet will provide you and your family with information and guidance on how "the law" of foreign countries and jurisdictions may affect you, how agreements between the United States and other governments determine when you may be subject to foreign jurisdiction, trial and possible imprisonment and what you should know about these matters as they may affect you during your on- or off-duty time.

The United States has agreements with many countries concerning the stationing of our forces in their territories. Generally speaking, the most important of these agreements now contain the essential protections and privileges embodied in the NATO Status of Forces Agreement. This booklet will concentrate on its provisions.

NATO STATUS OF
FORCES AGREEMENT

When the North Atlantic Treaty Organization came into existence in 1949, it was apparent that military personnel of one NATO country might be stationed in the
territory of another for extended periods of time. Thus, it
became desirable to establish uniform rules for handling
legal matters involving service members of one NATO
country stationed in another member country. This was
true not just for criminal cases, but also for civil claims,
taxes, customs and the like. Negotiations led to the sign-
ing of a NATO Status of Forces Agreement in June 1951.
After considerable debate, the U.S. Senate advised
ratification of the agreement in July 1953. This agreement

was ratified by the president during the same month.

The NATO Status of Forces Agreement defines the legal status of the armed forces of each member nation when stationed on the territory of another. It sets forth the rights, privileges and responsibilities of visiting forces and of individual members of such forces, including civilian employees and dependents of both military and civilian personnel.

Of the 16 NATO countries, 15 subscribe to the general provisions of the Status of Forces Agreement: the United States, Canada, the United Kingdom, Belgium, Denmark, France, Italy, Luxembourg, the Netherlands, Norway, Portugal, Greece, Turkey, the Federal Republic of Germany and Spain. In Iceland, the status of U.S. forces is governed by a separate agreement similar to the NATO formula. In some countries, such as Germany, Greece, the Netherlands, Turkey and Spain, there are supplemental agreements that confer additional benefits on members of the United States forces.

The laws and, indeed, the legal systems of these countries vary. How these differing laws and legal systems affect U.S. military and civilian personnel and their dependents concerns every American stationed overseas with our forces. Besides conferring limited privileges and immunities upon the members of United States forces, the NATO Status of Forces Agreement also expressly requires them to respect the laws of the country where they are assigned.

The agreement governs the relationship between our armed forces and foreign countries in matters of criminal jurisdiction, passport and visa regulations, taxes, claims, drivers licenses, airport regulations and other civil and legal matters.

You may want to obtain clarification as to your rights and obligations in your host country from your nearest overseas installation legal office. Frequently, there will be a local national attorney adviser on the staff who is thoroughly familiar with host country law as it applies to you. Also, your legal officers will know about "U.S. country representative instructions." These specific directives help you help the United States fulfill its treaty obligations. For example, you will find you must report all traffic incidents to your commander.

Much of what follows will be addressed in briefings at your new location. Take the time to become familiar with it now, and remember to visit your base legal office if ever you have a question about local law. You will find highly trained attorneys ready, willing and able to help you.

CRIMINAL JURISDICTION

A sovereign nation has jurisdiction, or legal authority, over most persons within its territory. However, under the NATO Status of Forces Agreement, the host country shares jurisdiction with the visiting armed forces' country in certain types of offenses.

The key to the legal status of an American service member overseas with the armed forces, if he or she is accused of a crime, is this matter of jurisdiction. Whether the accused will be tried by court-martial or stand trial in a foreign court depends upon which country has "exclusive" jurisdiction or a "primary" right to exercise "concurrent" jurisdiction, the United States or the host country.

Under the NATO Status of Forces Agreement, the United States has exclusive jurisdiction over certain categories of offenses. Some actions are punishable under the Uniform Code of Military Justice and other U.S. extraterritorial laws but not under the laws of the host country because the latter have not been violated. For example, evasion of U.S. income tax is an offense punishable by U.S. law but not the law of any other country. Violations such as unauthorized absence, desertion or refusal to obey a lawful order are purely military offenses, and U.S. military authorities have the sole right to try such cases.

The host country has exclusive jurisdiction over members of our military forces in cases where the offense is punishable by that country's laws, but not by the Uniform Code of Military Justice - for example, a customs violation.

The host country also has jurisdiction over civilian employees and dependents of military personnel or civilian employees. U.S. Supreme Court decisions in the late 1950s held that civilians are not subject to trial by court-martial during peacetime. Therefore, since United States military authorities have no effective criminal jurisdiction over civilians in peacetime, in most cases their offenses are punishable only by the laws of the host country.

In all other offenses, the NATO Status of Forces Agreement establishes a formula under which both nations have jurisdiction. Many crimes, such as murder, larceny and drunk driving, are crimes under the Uniform Code of Military Justice and under the host nation's laws. Thus, jurisdiction is shared or "concurrent" with both countries. The NATO Status of Forces Agreement establishes a formula for determining which country has the primary right to exercise jurisdiction over a particular offense.

PRIMARY JURISDICTION

The United States has the primary jurisdiction over its military personnel in three categories of offenses:

▶ Crimes solely against the property or security of the United States;

▶ Offenses rising out of any act or omission done in the performance of official duty;

▶ Crimes solely against the person or property of another U.S. service member, a civilian employee or a dependent.

In all other crimes, the host country retains the primary jurisdiction. If a U.S. service member, not in the performance of official duty, commits a crime against the person or property of a foreign national, local authorities have the primary right to bring him or her to trial. Unless the host country waives its primary jurisdiction, the accused will be prosecuted under the laws and procedures of that country's criminal justice system.

If convicted, the service member will be punished in accordance with the host country's laws.

WAIVER OF JURISDICTION

When an American military man or woman is accused of a crime over which the host country has the primary right to exercise jurisdiction, U.S. authorities may request a waiver of jurisdiction. That is, they may ask the local authorities to permit the U.S. authorities to exercise jurisdiction over the accused. A majority of these requests have been granted.

CUSTODY OF THE ACCUSED

When a service member is arrested and accused of a crime, which nation retains custody? This depends upon the provisions of the agreement applicable to the case. If a military member is arrested by U.S. military authorities for an offense over which the United States has the primary right to exercise jurisdiction, custody will remain with the United States. If local police arrest the military member for such an offense, they will turn the individual over to the American authorities. If a military member is arrested by U.S. authorities for an offense over which the host country has the primary right to exercise jurisdiction, the NATO Status of Forces Agreement allows the United States to retain custody until the suspect is officially charged with a violation of local law.

If foreign police arrest a U.S. service member for an offense over which the foreign country has the primary right to exercise jurisdiction, they are, in most instances, permitted to retain custody. They may, as a matter of courtesy, surrender the service member to American authorities.

In Germany, a supplemental agreement to the NATO Status of Forces Agreement grants custody to the United States until the accused is either acquitted or is convicted and begins to serve a sentence involving confinement. At that point, the convicted criminal will be transferred to a German prison. Other agreements with Greece, Portugal (for the Azores) and Spain permit the United States to retain custody until completion of all judicial proceedings.

RIGHTS OF THE ACCUSED

The NATO Status of Forces Agreement specifically guarantees an American military member, a civilian employee of the military or a dependent of either the right:

▶ To be accorded a prompt and speedy trial;

▶ To be informed in advance of the trial of the specific charge or charges made against him or her;

▶ To be confronted with the witnesses against him or her;

▶ To compel the appearance of witnesses in his or her favor;

▶ To have legal counsel of the individual's own choice for his or her defense;

▶ To have the services of a competent interpreter;

▶ To have a U.S. government representative present at the trial (when the rules of the court permit).

TRIAL OBSERVERS

When a U.S. service member, civilian employee of the U.S. armed forces or a dependent of either is tried for an offense by a foreign court in the country where stationed, he or she is entitled to have a U.S. government representative appointed to observe the trial, where the rules of the court permit. This observer, usually a lawyer of the armed forces, notes the manner in which the trial is conducted and makes a full report to the proper military authority.

This observer is not a participant in the defense and does not become involved in the proceedings. The observer may, however, advise defense counsel of the rights of the accused under applicable agreements.

The trial observer's report is reviewed by higher authorities to determine whether the accused was granted all safeguards guaranteed by the applicable Status of Forces Agreement and whether he or she received a fair trial. If a service member has been denied any guaranteed rights or has otherwise been unfairly prosecuted, U.S. authorities will take action through military or diplomatic channels to bring this fact to the attention of the host country authorities.

OTHER SAFEGUARDS

NOTIFICATION TO CONGRESS

When it consented to ratification of the NATO Status of Forces Agreement, the Senate passed a resolution requiring that Congress be notified:

▶ Whenever a foreign country refuses to waive jurisdiction in a case where it appears that the accused will not be protected because of the absence or denial of basic constitutional rights he or she would enjoy in the United States;

▶ If, during a trial, the accused is not granted the rights spelled out in the applicable Status of Forces Agreement.

PAYMENT OF EXPENSES

Congress has authorized the armed forces to pay the following expenses for U.S. military personnel, members of the civilian component and dependents tried in foreign courts:
- ► Counsel fees (for civilian counsel);
- ► Bail;
- ► Court costs;
- ► Other related trial expenses, such as an interpreter's fees.

This authority has been used in certain important or serious cases. It has enabled accused U.S. service personnel to hire private attorneys at government expense. Under very limited circumstances approved by the service secretary concerned, this authority may be used by U.S. service members, civilian employees and dependents to initiate civil litigation in the interest of the United States. In one instance, the Army hired civilian counsel to press the case of a service member who challenged a German businessman for violating German law against racial discrimination.

FINES, DAMAGES

The United States will not pay fines or damages for which an individual is liable.

REIMBURSEMENT

Service members, civilian employees and dependents will not be required to reimburse the United States for payments made for counsel fees, court costs and other trial expenses. However, should they willfully cause forfeiture of bail that has been posted for them, they will be required to reimburse the government for the amount of the bail.

DOUBLE JEOPARDY

A U.S. military member who has been tried by a foreign court cannot be tried again by court-martial for the same offense. However, he or she may be tried for a separate offense against the Uniform Code of Military Justice associated with the same incident. For example, if while absent without leave, a service member assaults a local national, he or she may be tried in a local court for the assault and may also be tried by court-martial for being absent without leave.

CONFINEMENT IN FOREIGN PRISONS

When a U.S. service member, civilian employee or dependent is confined in a foreign prison, he or she is not abandoned by the U.S. armed forces. His or her welfare and the protection of his or her rights continue to be the responsibility of the U.S. armed forces.
U.S. officials, to the extent permitted by agreement and local law, provide our personnel confined in foreign prisons with items and services they would receive if confined by American forces. These include legal assistance, medical and dental care, medicine, health and comfort items and supplemental food and clothing.

Service regulations require that the commanding officer or a named representative visit U.S. service members, civilian employees or dependents who are confined in a foreign prison at least once every 30 days. Conditions of confinement and the health and welfare of the prisoner will be observed and reported. Chaplains and medical officers will also visit periodically to provide for spiritual and physical needs.

If permission for these visits is denied without apparent good cause or if it appears that an individual is being mistreated or that the conditions of confinement are substandard, U.S. authorities will take steps to seek corrective action.

Except in unusual cases, no member of the U.S. armed forces confined in a foreign penal institution will be discharged or separated from the service until completion of the prison term and return to the United States.

Conditions in foreign prisons vary from country to country, just as they do in different states of the United States. Authorities who make periodic visits to prisons where Americans are confined make reports of their visits to assure that conditions are generally satisfactory.

STATUS OF U.S. FORCES
IN OTHER COUNTRIES

Since the NATO Status of Forces Agreement was first negotiated in the early 1950s, the United States has signed status of forces agreements with several other nations in which our forces are stationed. Most of them are patterned after the NATO Status of Forces Agreement.

These agreements with non-NATO countries protect the U.S. service member's basic rights as an American citizen. Variations from the NATO Status of Forces Agreement are generally favorable to American interests. One agreement may broaden the definition of civilian component. Another may provide for waiving the primary right to exercise jurisdiction more readily. A third may provide for more freely surrendering custody of an accused American service member to U.S. military authorities.

JAPAN

The status of forces agreement under Article VI of the Treaty of Mutual Cooperation and Security between the United States and Japan contains essentially the same provisions as the NATO Status of Forces Agreement. A major difference lies in the term "visiting force." Any U.S. service member present in Japan is considered a member of the "force." For example, a service member stationed in Korea but on leave in Japan comes under the agreement and is entitled to its benefits.

REPUBLIC OF THE PHILIPPINES

The Philippine Military Bases Agreement of 1947 was amended in 1965 and 1979 to include essentially the same criminal jurisdiction provisions as the NATO Status of Forces Agreement.

U.S. military authorities maintain custody of accused U.S. personnel until final judgment. At the request of the United States, Philippine authorities will consider the matter of waiving their primary right to exercise jurisdiction.

REPUBLIC OF KOREA

A status of forces agreement between the United States and the Republic of Korea went into effect in 1967. It, too, is essentially patterned after the NATO agreement.

Korean authorities have agreed to waive their primary right to exercise jurisdiction over U.S. service members, except in cases "of particular importance." An agreement has been made under which U.S. military authorities are not required to request a waiver in each case. Instead, they inform Korean authorities of offenses over which Korea has the primary right to exercise jurisdiction. If, within 15 days of this notification, Korean authorities do not notify U.S. military authorities that they intend to exercise their primary right to jurisdiction, the United States is free to exercise jurisdiction in the case.

The status of forces agreement with Korea guarantees an accused American service member the same rights spelled out in the NATO Status of Forces Agreement. In addition, other basic rights to which an accused is entitled are specified. These include:

▶ Protection from self-incrimination;

▶ Prohibition of cruel and unusual punishment;

▶ Prohibition against prosecution for an act that was not against the law at the time it was committed;

▶ Protection against legislative acts that punish an individual without judicial trial;

Protection against double jeopardy.

▶ Further, U.S. authorities retain custody of an American service member being prosecuted in a Korean court. The accused remains in American custody until all judicial proceedings, including any appeals, have been completed.

AUSTRALIA

Our status of forces agreement in effect with Australia since 1963 follows the pattern of the NATO Status of Forces Agreement.

PANAMA

One of our most recently negotiated status of forces agreements is the 1979 agreement with Panama, which implements the defense provisions of Article IV of the Panama Canal Treaty.

While this agreement is similar to the basic NATO Status of Forces Agreements, it has some distinctive differences. Panama has agreed to allow the United States primary jurisdiction over U.S. personnel for any criminal offense committed within U.S. defense sites. Additionally, when Panama has primary jurisdiction and intends to prosecute a U.S. service member, the agreement grants the United States the right to hold the service member in custody until the completion of all judicial proceedings. An exception to this rule of custody applies for five major criminal offenses (murder, robbery, rape, drug trafficking or crimes against the security of Panama). Here the agreement allows Panama to retain custody of an accused.

SPAIN

Another recent status of forces agreement is the Agreement of Defense and Economic Cooperation with Spain. Under it, the provisions of the NATO Status of Forces Agreement apply, as supplemented, in Spain.

In cases where Spain has the primary right to exercise jurisdiction, the Spanish government has agreed to waiver primary jurisdiction upon request, except in cases of particular importance to it. In addition, custody of an American who is being prosecuted in a Spanish court is entrusted to U.S. military authorities until the conclusion of all judicial proceedings.

PORTUGAL

The technical agreement in implementation of the defense agreement between the United States and Portugal applies the NATO Status of Forces Agreement to U.S. bases in the Azores. Similar to the Spanish agreement, it provides more favorable criminal jurisdiction treatment for American service members in areas of waiver of primary jurisdiction to the United States and custody.

LEGAL STATUS OF OFFICES OF DEFENSE COOPERATION AND MILITARY MISSIONS

Besides having armed forces stationed in foreign countries under treaties for mutual defense, the United States has, through separate agreements, military missions and offices of defense cooperation in a number of countries. Most of these offices are small, their main job being to implement U.S. international security assistance programs — in particular, foreign military sales in that country.

Each of these specialized missions and offices is established under an agreement between the United States and the country concerned. The legal status of Office of Defense Cooperation and mission personnel varies from country to country, and their criminal jurisdiction status is subject to the agreements with the countries concerned.

In general, personnel receive the diplomatic privileges of the embassy, of which by agreement they are a part; the United States in many cases has exclusive jurisdiction over mission personnel under country agreements. Members of military missions and Office of Defense Cooperation groups should consult their commanding officers as to their exact legal status in the country in which they are assigned.

STATUS OF CIVILIAN EMPLOYEES AND DEPENDENTS

In the late 1950s, the U.S. Supreme Court held that civilians are not subject to trial by court-martial in peacetime. Thus, except for other U.S. extraterritorial legislation of limited applicability (such as U.S. espionage or income tax laws), the United States cannot exercise criminal jurisdiction over military dependents or civilian employees and their dependents living in foreign countries. These individuals fall under the jurisdiction of the host country; their offenses are punishable by the laws of that country. However, they are entitled to the applicable safeguards guaranteed by the various status of forces agreements.

If a local commander determines that suitable corrective action under existing administrative regulations can be taken, foreign authorities may be requested to refrain from exercising their jurisdiction.

If such a request is denied and it further appears possible that the accused may not obtain a fair trial, the United States will seek to resolve the matter through diplomatic channels.

Service regulations direct military commanders to assist civilian employees and dependents in the custody of foreign authorities or confined in foreign penal institutions. In cooperation with diplomatic authorities, commanders will, insofar as possible, assure that such civilians receive the same treatment, rights and support as military personnel.

STATUS OF FORCES AGREEMENTS
AND FOREIGN CLAIMS

When large numbers of Americans are stationed in a foreign country, incidents inevitably arise that result in civil claims against the U.S. military forces. Effective and timely settlement of claims does much to maintain good international relations and to resolve outstanding criminal charges. It also makes the presence of American military forces more acceptable to the people of a foreign nation.

To avoid friction, provisions are made in the status of forces agreements for the prompt settlement of claims arising out of the activities of our armed forces.

U.S. service regulations authorize the administrative settlement of meritorious claims that are caused by a member or civilian employee of U.S. forces or that result from non-combat activities of those forces. U.S. military authorities administer the entire foreign claims program so as to take full advantage of its favorable impact on the foreign relations of the United States.

Under the NATO Status of Forces Agreement, a foreign national's claim against a U.S. service member acting in an official capacity is processed by the host country. The host country determines whether the claim is to be paid and the amount to be paid. The host country pays the claimant and then seeks reimbursement from the United States for 75 percent of the amount paid. The agreement provides that the host country will pay 25 percent of the cost of settlement.

When a claim against the United States forces arises out of an act not done in the performance of official duty, the host country investigates the claim. Its recommendation about settlement is forwarded to U.S. authorities, who will consider whether payment should be made. If the United States elects to pay the claim, it bears the entire cost of payment. The service member involved is not required to reimburse the U.S. government but may be subject to some form of legal or administrative action, depending upon the circumstances involved.

On the other hand, a U.S. service member may be sued as an individual for damages, and a foreign court may hand down a judgment against him or her, where the act or omission was not done in the performance of official duty. In such a case, payment of damages is the full responsibility of the individual service member, unless the United States has already made a payment that has been accepted by the claimant in full settlement of the claim.

If a civil suit for damages is brought against an individual U.S. service member for an act done in the performance of official duty, he or she should report the fact immediately to the commander of the installation as well as to the command judge advocate.

ADDITIONAL PRIVILEGES AND OBLIGATIONS

The NATO Status of Forces Agreement contains several additional privileges and obligations for U.S. personnel stationed in a country party to the agreement. Similar privileges and obligations frequently apply in other countries where U.S. forces are stationed.

THESE PRIVILEGES INCLUDE:

▶ Exemption from foreign taxes on their tangible personal property and on salaries paid them by the U.S. government;

▶ The right to import, free of duty, furniture and personal effects at the time of their first arrival for duty

34

or at the time of the first arrival of their dependents to join them. They may also import, free of duty, automobiles for their personal use and that of their dependents;

▶ Host country acceptance, without additional fee or test, of military driving permits and drivers licenses issued to military personnel by any U.S. state or the District of Columbia;

▶ Exemption of members of the armed forces from passport and visa regulations. This does not apply to civilians or dependents.

THESE OBLIGATIONS INCLUDE:

▶ Obtaining permission of host country authorities to sell locally any item imported duty-free into the country;

▶ Compliance with foreign exchange regulations;

▶ The duty to respect the laws of the host country.

SOME POINTS TO BEAR IN MIND

A sovereign nation has the right to exercise jurisdiction over persons in its territory. All persons in a country - including military personnel - unless granted diplomatic or other legal immunity, are subject to that country's laws.

A status of forces agreement defines the legal status of

the armed forces of one nation when stationed in the territory of another.

Under a status of forces agreement, the host country shares jurisdiction over military personnel of a "visiting force."

The host country has jurisdiction, as a general rule, over civilian employees and dependents of military or civilian personnel.

The United States will pay the trial expenses for a U.S. service member, civilian employee or dependent being tried for a crime by a foreign court.

If an American service member, civilian employee or dependent is confined in a foreign penal institution, the United States will seek to assure treatment and protections similar to those accorded personnel confined in U.S. military facilities.

A U.S. military member or civilian employee can be sued in the civil courts of a foreign nation and be liable for damages for his or her non-duty acts. Dependents may also be sued in foreign civil courts.

All Americans abroad have the duty to respect the laws of the nations they visit and in which they are stationed.

The Secretary of Defense
Washington

November 1988

YOU AND THE LAW
OVERSEAS
(DOD GEN-37C)
This official Department of
Defense publication is for
the use of personnel in the
military services.

www.ingramcontent.com/pod-product-compliance
Lightning Source LLC
Chambersburg PA
CBHW070935290526
45795CB00003B/1033